Responses to
The New Creation in Male and Female

David's unique perspective on the believer will empower you to a higher calling of responsibility to fulfill God's original intent.
—Dr Aaron Winter, Hearts of Fire Intl., Washington, USA

David O'Brien's new book "New Creation in Male and Female" creates a vivid picture of all of humanity: how the lure of seeking for something we already have began; and what to do about it: how to enter a new life; no longer enslaved by the lure of our common enemy. Powerful!
—Richard Matteson, Christ Love Ministries Intl., RI, USA

What a wonderful read. Full of Light and Life and Truth. Powerful revelations from the Holy Spirit in its beautiful simplicity. I loved it! I saw myself in Adam, I saw myself in Eve. It felt like it was written directly for me. Yet, I know that is how God had it written for each and every one of us. I really do highly recommend it. It truly blessed me.
—Charlene Sober, California, USA

I recommend this book. It is an easy read. I love the way this is worded, there was absolutely no judgement but an understanding regarding some of the "why's" you may have about Adam and Eve. 'Helped to understand the love God has for us. 'Also helped to understand the New Creation which was explained in an easy-to-understand way. Enjoy!!
—Natasha Rowles, Brisbane, Australia

ii

Book 1 of the
SUPERNATURAL ROYALTY-ED
Series

The New Creation in Male & Female

David O'Brien

Scripture quotations from the following Bible versions:

The New King James Version. Copyright © 1982 by Thomas Nelson, Inc. Used by permission. All rights reserved.
The NEW AMERICAN STANDARD BIBLE®, Copyright © 1960,1962,1963,1968,1971,1972,1973,1975,1977, 1995, 2020 by The Lockman Foundation. Used by permission.
The Holy Bible, English Standard Version copyright 2001, 2007, 2011, 2016 by Crossway Books and Bibles, a Publishing Ministry of Good News Publishers. Used by permission. All rights reserved.

Abbreviations as follows:
NKJV – New King James Version
NASB – New American Standard Bible
ESV – English Standard Version

Literal translation is often added within Scripture references, with brackets: { and }.

Blue Diamond Bookhouse
www.BlueDiamondBookhouse.com

www.TheBondageBreaker.com

Therefore, if anyone is in Christ, A NEW CREATION; old things have passed away; behold, all things have become new.
—2Corinthians 5:17 NKJV, The Bible

Dedication

To the Disciples of Jesus. To those just charting their path, to those who need refreshing, and to those desiring their Father's training and help. I salute you. I love you. And I have dug your spiritual enemy's grave for you, through this book and this series.

Restoring the Kingdom lost:

"The Kingdom of Heaven" =
The Reign of "The God of Heaven" (Daniel 2:44)
(not the place called "heaven")

"Christ / Messiah" =
The Anointed King:
Chosen, Appointed & Empowered by God to rule & serve

"Church" =
The Legislature:
God's special selected People, called out of the world to rule

Contents

Let His Kingdom Fill Your Thoughts

For years I've wanted to write this series for God's People, covering many areas relevant to the ROYALTY we have as God's Children:

- New Covenant Identity
- True Spirituality
- Love
- Distinctiveness
- Freedom
- The Power of an Image
- How to Deal with the Media Cliff
- God's Design for Kingdom Marriages
  And
- Supernaturally Thriving K-12
- Fulfilling Your Royal Destiny – Reaching Your Brightest Shine

We think differently. We are different. But so many of God's People do not know the freedom and wisdom and understanding available to us. It's like a very small beam of light in a dark place.

It is time for that to change. The sewer will be illuminated, by Fire. And the dragon will be extinguished and immobilized. Good News will get into the hearts and souls of God's people, as hot healing oil.

Within the royalty that you possess in the Kingdom of God, as the King's sons and daughters, is everything you need for the BEST life on earth.

Let His divine, supernatural royalty fill your thinking, through this book and this series.

Chapter 1
In the Garden...

Adam was not deceived by the serpent. He bit the forbidden fruit based on something else. For him, it was not out of deception.[1]

In the Garden, Eve spoke to the serpent and listened to him. She gave up what she had, for what he offered her. She was tricked.[2] And Adam was there. She offered the fruit to him, and he then had a choice to consider. Do I obey God and *refuse* my wife, or do make sure I keep my wife by disobeying God?

Her image grew huge in his eyes. Her beauty. And he laid aside the glory of God, not for the fruit, but for her. That was the glory he was looking at and being tempted by. It was not the fruit or any of the lies the enemy used on her—it was *the glory of woman,* the brightness of the one God had made for him. That's what he went for. It's what he gave everything for.

How must God have felt, to be replaced in the desire of man by his gift to man? God's name is "Jealous." And the pain of the nails going into Jesus' hands was to correct this, to set males free from the idolatry of the image of woman, among other things, to KILL the nature of Adam, and bury it fully, for those in The Anointed King ("Christ").

Then three days later, at the dawn of the third day, in The Anointed King, the New Creation was born of God. We rose with him, into newness of Life. This new realm is so different than the old one, so different than fallen Man's way of existence. This was the beginning of the New Creation. The cross and resurrection were necessary to bring it about.

Now the new world is what we make of it, by Love. We were resurrected in The Anointed King with the nature of Love, and its POWER. We can raise the dead now, in our time. And we can communicate with the old nature people and give them new Life. We

---

[1] See 1Timothy 2:14, The Bible
[2] 1Timothy 2:14

1

make all things beautiful, through our transformation into His image.

We are like him now. We are The Anointed King's fragrance now, in the midst of a pained and crooked generation. We are transformed healers. We go to people and bring them up. We are the salt of our Father, to heal the wounds of those dwelling in darkness and bring light and illumination to them, as fire. By the blood Jesus shed and the righteousness he made us into, we can walk and delight those around us—all of them—whether they admit it publicly or not. We are their warm oasis.

Light is never afraid of darkness.

Receiving the Word protects us from any old, dysfunctional ways of thinking and living. It protects us and helps us walk a new way, while erroneous thoughts are purified in our souls by fire. God wants us to go up on his Word like a ladder, step by step, with both confidence and cautiousness—our protection for the right hand and the left. He's preparing us for our grand, destiny service, to go far with his Good News for others. That same Good News that medicates and heals you, will lift others as you go and communicate it to them.

God's remedy for Adam and Eve was not condemnation. "The soul that sins shall die," yes. But God's plan was "redemption," substitution. Jesus took on their nature and sins and death, so we could live through him, as part of the New Creation.

We are no longer estranged from God as orphans. We are connected. We have a Father who is Light. We were born of him. We are *like* him. We are here, among the Old Creation, to shine as Lights in the midst of it. We give them access to our Home, through the Word of God that we share with them.

We are no longer of Adam.

We are of The Anointed King. We are of God. We no longer have Adam's deficiencies or Eve's. We do not bear their identity anymore. In The Anointed King we escape all of that. We are, like the risen Jesus, Life-giving spirits now (1Cor 15:45-48). Anything that used to prey on Adam's race and thwart it, is destroyed by the Life of God that comes out of us now, as we stand and serve.

Adam took one bite of the fruit, not for the fruit, but for the woman. Then he lost his glory; he became flesh. His spirit died in relation to God, being disconnected from him. And he realized he was physically naked.

But The Anointed King died for his Bride, to clothe her. The males of the New Creation no longer bow in worship of the glory of women.

2

We stand in honor of them, give them unconditional love, and clothe them with our own cloaks. Our job is to clothe them, whenever need be. To bring them in from the cold and tell them they're accepted. To lay down our lives for them. We kill our own souls/desires, to save them. We are *like God*. We are The Anointed King on the earth—his Body. And we voluntarily serve women. No blame. No idolatry. Love and covering and healing.

Jesus already did the work to save all. Now those that are of the New Creation—in Him—love and bring what he did to light for all. We are connected to the Source; his light streams through us as through fiber-optic cables, and we *pour* love and living Truth into people.

That love and living, liquid Truth turns the lights on inside of people, so that they see according to God, they see things his way, from his perspective. It's like they have a hidden contact lens that's really a video screen, for their eyes, which shows them his perspective and what he wants them to see.

Chapter 2
Freedom Had a Cost

So God's beauty, the glory he gave the woman, was twisted into an appealing offer of idolatry, a tool of seduction against the man. That was a powerful and persuasive offer. For Adam to withstand that, he would have to take his eyes off of it and put them on a source of greater glory—of light being poured out to him, of God inside of that light. He could've done this.

For Adam to bypass all of that glory, the glory of woman, he would've naturally felt he was losing something—the glorious gift God had given him. He would have had to kill the desire for it, inside of himself, to go beyond and worship God alone. That would've felt like an inner crucifixion of something that his soul found dear.

[Matthew 16:24-26 NKJV, literal added[3]] Then Jesus said to His disciples, "If anyone desires to come after Me, let him deny himself, and take up his cross, and follow Me. 25 "For whoever desires to save his {soul} will {kill} it, but whoever {kills} his {soul} for My sake will find it. 26 "For what profit is it to a man if he gains the whole world, and loses his own soul? Or what will a man give in exchange for his soul [that is, to purchase his soul back]?

Killing his soul is exactly what Adam did not do. Instead, he saved this desire of his soul and lost track of the path he was on with God. So what came next? He fell terribly to the earth.

Adam and Eve were created as spirit first, then breathed by God into the earthly bodies God formed for them (Gen 2:7[4]). They were not primarily physical. They *never* could have imagined their origin was from a monkey, a random explosion, or anything like that. But all of the

---

[3] Literal added, as in many others, notated with brackets: { and }.
[4] The Hebrew for "the breath of life" here is actually, "the breath of lives" or "spirit of lives."

sudden, they became earthly, somewhat similar to the animals.

The dirt. The dirt is what Adam's body was formed of. And now all he could see was that level of living. *THAT* was painful. He was a king, a representative of GOD'S Kingdom which is invisible to the physical eye. They had been given the task of ruling on the earth, exercising royal dominion. But now they were shut out of the spirit and forced to survive.

The physical was the smallest part of them. They were made spirit, soul, and body. But now, they were shut into the physical realm.

They hadn't even known that they were physically naked. The light they took in was primarily spiritual and so rich and bright that they couldn't see their physical nakedness. In fact, when Adam took the fruit in order to keep Eve, he was looking not at her physical body—the lowest form of her glory. He was looking at the real her. She was light, and she was glowing. It wasn't her soul that he was so impressed with; that was nice but still developing, and was not her essence. No, he was most impressed with her spirit. And all of the sudden, their spirits *lost* the glory of God. And they were reduced to being merely physical.

God had said, "In the day you eat of it, you will surely die." This is what happened to their spirits that day. And it left them physical, able primarily to think on earthly things, unable to connect with or relate to God spiritually anymore. Immediately they knew that they were naked physically, and they tried to remedy that.

Now consider Eve's situation. She was tricked by the serpent's cunning. But her biggest mistake was *listening to him at all in the first place.* Adam was there, at least part of the time,[5] but didn't seem to help, or at least he failed to lead. Now Eve had eaten the fruit. Remember, she was deceived. She believed the lie that God had lied to her, and that this new way was good for her. She inadvertently joined with the enemy, aligning herself on his team, then turned toward her husband to tempt him.

Again, she did not know fully what she was doing. She did not know the influence of her matchless beauty and glory on Adam. She just wanted to make sure he didn't leave her. She wanted to secure him with her, for her.

Getting him to stay with her was a bit tricky. He was not deceived by the serpent. What incentive could she give? What was the most glorious thing on earth? *She was.* So she offered herself, to keep him. She "gave the fruit to her husband, who was with her." But he was not deceived like she had been. And he had never disobeyed God. So she

---

[5] Genesis 3:6

had to persuade him to eat it.

Thankfully, thankfully Jesus came to earth and paid the price of redemption—the cost to buy humanity back from evil and create a reset. He did this to create a People who could now be upright on the earth. The Old Nature was too far gone. In fact, even the slightest contamination had power to ruin the whole thing.[6] It had to be replaced with the New. That is, "The Anointed King in you."[7]

When the Anointed King died, it was not only Jesus dying, but all those who would be put *into* him. They died there too; they were buried too; and they were raised into *glorious* new Life too—the Life of the risen, Son of God.[8] This is "newness of Life." It is available NOW. It is actually far greater than what Adam and Eve had at first. Now, by receiving what God says about Jesus, and acting on it, you are birthed by God, into NEW LIFE.

[2 Corinthians 5:17 NKJV, emphasis mine] Therefore, if anyone [is] in Christ [or the risen, Anointed King], A NEW CREATION; old things have passed away; behold, all things have become new.

You're new. If you're in The Anointed King, you are new. So you are no longer bound to the mistakes of fallen humanity. Your operating system is new—you have a new heart, a new spirit. You are, once again, connected to God by your spirit, and you can have a completely satisfying, one-on-one relationship with him again.

Also, your new nature is The Anointed King.

[Galatians 2:20 NKJV] "I have been crucified with [The Anointed King]; it is no longer I who live, but [The Anointed King] lives in me; and the [life] which I now live in the flesh I live [by] faith [of] the Son of God, who loved me and gave Himself for me.

That "The Anointed King in you," that new, born-again spirit, has God's nature in it because you were born of God. Your new nature now has the DNA signature of God in it—the exact DNA of your Father, who is God. You carry his nature now, as his offspring.[9] Your nature now, is one of righteousness and distinctiveness ("holiness"), of Love,

---

[6] James 2:10
[7] Colossians 1:27
[8] Romans 6:3-11
[9] 1John 3:1-2

peace and Truth. You've been freed from the old nature (the "Old Man/Old Adam").[10] This was accomplished by the death, burial and resurrection of God's Son, Jesus, with you inside of him!

[Ephesians 4:24 NKJV] …the new man [that is, the New Creation/New Nature] was created according to God, in true righteousness and holiness.

[John 1:12-13 NKJV] But as many as received Him [Jesus], to them He gave the right to become children of God, to those who believe {unto} His name: 13 who were born, not of blood, nor of the will of the flesh, nor of the will of man, but of God.

You escape the Old Nature and all its trappings, which befall both men and women, by being in the New Man, with its New Nature. *In this way* you have escaped "the corruption that's in the world through [strong desire]" (2Pe 1:4)!! And how is this activated in your life? By "true knowledge," or more literally, "supernatural knowledge"[11]:

[2 Peter 1:2-3 ESV] May grace and peace be multiplied to you in the {supernatural knowledge} of God and of Jesus our Lord. 3 His divine power has granted to us all things that pertain to life and godliness, through the {supernatural knowledge} of him who called {us his} own glory and excellence,

As Jesus, who is the head of the New Creation, instructed:

[John 8:31-32 NASB] So Jesus was saying to those Jews who had believed Him, "If you continue in My word, [then] you are truly My disciples [or "students"]; 32 and you will know the truth, and the truth will set you free."

---

10 Romans 6:6-7

11 Gr., "epignosis" = literally, "knowledge above experiential knowledge." This is spiritual knowledge or "true knowledge" that comes directly from God (see Jn 6:45). Also in 2 Peter 1:2-3, quoted next

Chapter 3
What Happened to Eve?

She ate the fruit. The goal was to obtain knowledge, a special kind that God had allegedly held back from her. She would not die, but she would become "like God," the enemy said. She looked at the fruit, examined it, and it looked *physically* attractive to her. It also *seemed good* to her, to "make one wise." It looked like good food for the body too. So she made "her" decision but didn't realize the force of influence she had connected herself to.

Because she had listened to the enemy's voice, she was actually under his deception. She was stupefied and in a lull-like trance, at that time. She was under the serpent's poisonous deception but unaware of it.

What was in that fruit? Perhaps nothing, physically. But it represented a cross-over, from trusting God and his Words and warnings, to trusting the deceiver. Who we trust in is who influences and affects us. So by eating the apple, at the enemy's suggestion, she was plugging into the enemy and becoming a "sponge" to soak up his lies.

She trusted in a counterfeit light, which is actually harmful to the eyes and lacks the complete substance of the real One. It does look like light and can be used to get around and operate, but it is not the real Light. Afterward, when the True Light came, it caused her to hide, and she saw herself for the first time as mere flesh. Her spirit had died.

When Eve, stupefied, took the fruit, as I said, she was under like a spell. That power—which we call witchcraft or manipulation today—came directly through the serpent's words. It was packaged inside of his words. She was woozy. However, this did not make her fully innocent.

Adam received the greater punishment since he was not deceived, as Scripture reveals. But we have to understand and dissect Eve's mistake, so that we are alert and don't make it again. SHE LISTENED TO THE SERPENT!

Stop and think for a moment about the multitude in Jerusalem who

9

rejected Jesus when he came in on a donkey (in fulfilment of true prophecy). Why did they eventually reject him and shout out in a mad stupor, "crucify, crucify!"? Scripture reveals it was because their leaders[12]—they were connected to enemy through the wrong voice, like Eve was through the serpent.

Eve befriended him and had a conversation with him. That was her fatal flaw. Eating the fruit was a predictable result. 'Like going to a quack-doctor for advice and as a result, taking poisonous medicine, the cause of her mistake was getting familiar with the enemy.

The serpent was "friendly." He is the friendly form of the evil one. He showed himself as being weak, much, much weaker than her, so that she would give him a moment "to chat." But his *words,* which carried his perspective, were deadly. He did have spikes and a painful, terror side, but he was hiding that, showing himself to be innocent and weak and pitiable—until she ate. Then he could grow huge and show himself as the dragon, with ravenous delight and desire for her in his eyes. This is the way of the devil, the enemy.

Now, after Eve ate the fruit, she was fully subdued by that enemy. Through trickery, he brought her to where he could attack her with all of his power. But the man, Adam didn't see that yet. All he saw at that point was the woman—her exquisite glory. The enemy was behind her, using her as a "human shield" so to speak, hiding himself behind her and offering her to the man. She gave Adam to eat also, and He folded under her beauty and glory.

The enemy was behind Eve, propping her up to Adam, with all of her feminine beauty. Her pure light was shining, and the dragon behind her was powering her to do what she was doing. He had his spike in her back—as the dragon now, not as the serpent. And he was exerting all of his power and false glory to have her shine before Adam. Adam didn't see the enemy at that point as he was hiding behind Eve's glory. Adam only saw the beautiful, good glory of the woman.

So what was the enemy doing to Eve? At that point, she was like a dummy-idol. He had subdued her and could use her. But how?

Eve had made a mistake. She had come under deception and disobeyed, by what she thought was her own, clever reasoning. When she ate the fruit, she found it not pleasant, not good for food, not sweet, not easy to eat, not making her greater or wiser.

---

[12] Mark 15:11

And then the enemy began to accuse her. This was private—between she and the enemy. That same enemy that had been communicating as a weak, friendly snake began to shout at her and breath fire out at her and intimidate and scare her. She got scared; he used intimidation to steer her on the path he wanted: fear of harm, fear of being defective and different now than Adam, fear of being vulnerable and alone. She saw herself as a mess now, as a "hot mess," as potentially undesirable (though she wasn't). Her emotions and nervous system were running at a million miles a minute: "What if I am alone—no God and no Adam?"

Remember, the serpent is the father of lies. He had many of them for her. The enemy transformed back into a serpent again, now a big one, and transferred these lies into Eve's mind as with a microchip, in a moment. She held and harbored these thoughts in her heart as secrets, keeping them from Adam. But they grew in her. She didn't look the same to herself in the mirror, so to speak. She saw herself as really, really ugly, as death with beautiful hair. She got desperate and tried to cleanse herself, but she was not the same anymore. She had to poo now, so to speak, and it was going to stink.

She tried to make herself look more beautiful, but she felt only like a "hot mess." Adam was watching some of this but not understanding and not able to get involved. Her internal mirror was like a source of terror for her, because she saw herself as death—ugly, despite her feminine beauty. She got to the end of herself, not knowing what to do.

Now I want to share with you about the New-Creation Daughters of God. They are much different from Eve's fallen state, the basic state of old creation women. They have a supernatural, bullet-proof vest on, called righteousness, that was given to them. It protects them from the enemy's accusation. His worst spew *cannot* penetrate that armor. They can just smile, from a much higher and more dominant place than the enemy will ever attain, knowing that they wear the royal, glorious crown and garments, bought by the blood of Jesus. And they are beautiful *in every way*. When the dragon recognizes he cannot penetrate that armor, he turns away from the New Creation in women. He knows there is nothing he can do.

Chapter 4
The Failure of Adam

[John 8:3-7 NKJV] Then the scribes and Pharisees brought to Him a woman caught in adultery. And when they had set her in the midst, 4 they said to Him, "Teacher, this woman was caught in adultery, in the very act. 5 "Now Moses, in the law, commanded us that such should be stoned. But what do You say?" 6 This they said, testing Him, that they might have [something] of which to accuse Him. But Jesus stooped down and wrote on the ground with [His] finger, as though He did not hear. 7 So when they continued asking Him, He raised Himself up and said to them, *"He who is without sin among you, let him throw a stone at her first."*

We've talked about what happened to Eve. Now let's look at the failure of Adam. In addition to idolizing her, he *failed to cover* Eve.

[1 Peter 4:8 NKJV] "…love will cover a multitude of sins."

Eve was down. She had been shot and was down for the count. And we know that Adam took the attractive bait offered him to also accept the fruit. At that moment, he wanted Eve more than he wanted God who made him. He was tempted to think he could have both—both disobedience to God *and* God. He was so impressed with the woman's image. Not just her body, mind you. He was much more focused on her essence. And she was inviting him to worship her.

And he did. He gave up the *glory of God* for a small piece of cheese (that is, the bait). In reality, no matter *how* glorious Eve was, she was made from the image of God; he's where her glory came from. God is the substance, the real thing! Adam had *God*. But he chose Eve. In reality, she was bait at that point. He wanted to devour that bait. He wanted to *have her* for himself. If he had kept God in his #1 spot, he would've had both God *and* her. And he could've covered her wrongdoing.

Let me share with you that God's ultimate judgment was against the serpent, not against Adam and Eve. Their judgment was temporary, but the serpent would be totally crushed, by an Offspring of Eve. Do you see the honor given to Eve by God, as a covering for her?

Why? Because God is merciful. The Father "delights in mercy" (Micah 7:18). They were afraid and hid from him because their vision had been skewed. The real him, loves mercy, loves compassion, forgives and saves people. That's the True God.

So what did Adam do that furthered his failure? What did he do when God asked if he ate the fruit? He *accused* Eve.

[Genesis 3:12 NKJV] 12 Then the man said, "The woman whom You gave to be with me, she gave me of the tree, and I ate."

This was a painful blow to the woman's inner being. Not only the dragon, but now the man, her companion, was pointing a finger at her! She was facing execution, judgment, condemnation. I can see her in her inner being gasping for air, tears escaping from her eyes. Where could she go, to whom could she turn. She was formed from the side of the man, and he forsook her. She was afraid of God now also!

But God, whose nature is actually Love, who shows mercy like no other, gave her a promise. It had nothing to do with her deserving anything. He *loved her*. So he clothed her and her husband, with animal skins, and he said to the serpent:

[Genesis 3:15, 21 NKJV] ...I will put enmity between you and the woman, and between your seed and her Seed; He shall bruise your head, and you shall bruise His heel." ... 21 Also for Adam and his wife the LORD God made tunics of skin, and clothed them.

Their mistakes had consequences, serious ones. But notice how God was taking care of them and redeeming them in the midst of that. He foretold the fact that Eve's Seed would destroy their enemy-accuser, and then he clothed them with leather—from the first death of an animal—a *sacrifice* to cover them and alleviate their shame. This was a picture of the sacrifice of Messiah, the Anointed King. He was that Seed of Eve who would come as our ultimate help and clothe us in His sacrifice, after stomping on the head of Satan.

God was revealing his master-mercy plan that he had all along, from "before the foundation of the world." It was to redeem fallen man and put those who believe inside of The Anointed King, where we would become the new and completely clean, New Creation.

[2 Corinthians 5:17-19 NKJV] Therefore, if anyone [is] in [The Anointed King], [he is] a new creation; old things have passed away; behold, all things have become new. 18 Now all things [are] of God, who has reconciled us to Himself through Jesus [The Anointed King], and has given us the ministry of reconciliation, 19 that is, that God [is] in [The Anointed King] reconciling the world to Himself, [not counting their sins against them]…

Now look at this verse to understand—let your eyes now be opened—to what God is really like:

[Romans 5:15-16 NKJV] But the free gift [is] not like the offense. For if by the one man's [that is, Adam's] offense many died, much more the grace of God and the gift by the grace of the one Man, Jesus [The Anointed King], abounded to many. 16 And the gift [is] not like [that which came] through the one who sinned. For the judgment [which came] from one [offense resulted] in condemnation, but the free gift [which came] from many offenses [resulted] in justification.

Death followed Adam and Eve's sins. God had said it would, and his word *cannot* be broken. It was a reality he warned them about. However, that did not change his love for them or his nature of Love. It merely directed his Love in such a way that he brought a *sacrifice*, One who would take all of the sin into himself and suffer the penalty for it all. In this way, God and that One would set them free.

And when did God do that? After there were "many offenses." Not just the first few sins Adam and Eve did, but a vast *multitude* of them— that's when God's great mercy was shown. His generosity, completely undeserved, was given to fallen humanity without restraint.

[Romans 5:6-8 NKJV] For when we were still without strength, in due time [The Anointed King] died for the ungodly. 7 For scarcely for a righteous man will one die; yet perhaps for a good man someone would even dare to die. 8 But God demonstrates His own love toward us, in that while we were still sinners, [The Anointed King] died for us.

Do you know the parable of "the prodigal son," of Luke Chapter 15? The father's son was away from home, hungry and wishing he could eat the food of the pigs he was feeding. This was all because of his own foolishness. But what was that father doing? That father was a picture Jesus painted for us of God the Father. What was he doing? Was he mad??? He was looking out of his window, longing for his son's return. He was compassionate and had deep mercy for his son.

God had the same compassion on you and I too.

Adam and Eve were both blinded by their own guilt, to think that God was coming to judge them. No, He was coming to *save* them, despite their mistake and its consequences! His love for them was constant. He was coming to judge the serpent: The Messiah would surely come now, by the Word of God that cannot be broken, and crush that devil's head.

This happened when Jesus came into the world, supernaturally born of the virgin Mary—the Son of God. He came to die, to do what Adam did not do. Jesus came to take the rock thrown by Adam at Eve, to take the accusations the dragon spewed on both of them. He came to take all of the righteous judgment of God against sin, for them. To freely bring us back to God as innocent, Jesus took the fall.

Jesus took the pain. He took the blame and the shame. The innocent was sacrificed for the guilty, to open our eyes to what the Father is really like and allow us to walk back over to him, by the work of Jesus' on his cross. The Father accepted Eve. He accepts all of her daughters who come to him freely now. He accepts the men, fallen desperately like Adam. And he fixes your face—the caking, the worms, the ugliness—he blasts it clean. ☺

He cleanses your inner being. The cleansing happens from above. Your inner being is completely cleansed out by Him.

He lets you dip a toe into his hot, healing and restoring, natural spring for you. And he gives you a new day. The dawning of a new day is given to you.

There is a transfer of power now available to your spirit. After Jesus' body laid in a tomb for three days, the glory of God raised him from the dead, and the Father gave him the greatest glory. Jesus is seated on the highest throne now, as Lord of all. And remember what he is for you: the Sacrifice. His nature on that throne is Love and mercy.

And here's the GOOD NEWS for those who haven't known Jesus: he is inviting you up to his throne with him now, to sit and reign with him. All sins forgiven, all acceptance given, he will accept you into himself and his Kingdom, and you will become part of the New Life—

a part of the New Creation.

[Romans 10:9, 11, 13 NKJV] if you confess [that is, "acknowledge"] with your mouth the Lord Jesus and believe in your heart that God has raised Him from the dead, you will be saved. ... 11 For the Scripture says, "Whoever believes on Him will not be put to shame." ... 13 For "whoever calls on the name of the LORD shall be saved."

If you haven't actually known Jesus, call on him now to save you. Acknowledge him verbally as the Lord of your life, and he will save you. That is your new beginning. You pass from death to Life.

Also, miraculous healing comes to your body now too, if you need it. Take your right hand and put it on wherever needs healing right now. In the authority of Jesus who sent me to you through this book, as you do that, I now tell that part of your body: "revive and work properly." Now get up and try out that part of your body. *Whatever* you could not do, do, and you will see the miracle!

Then look at yourself because if you have made Jesus The Anointed King your Lord, you are a new being now, fully forgiven & totally new.

The next step for you is immersion in water, in Jesus' Name (traditionally called, "water baptism"). A fellow believer can do it for you; they just dunk you in the water. You are identifying with Jesus, publicly with this extremely powerful, spiritual act. You leave behind the old to walk in your new life now, with Him.

There is also something in Scripture for you, called "immersion in the Holy Spirit." And there is the Word of God to begin receiving regularly; this is your spiritual food. There is the distinctive community—God's People of true faith. For more on this, I recommend to you my teaching, "First Steps."

18

Chapter 5
In Newness of Life Now

Jesus ended the old creation man by his death, for all who believe into him. He was rescuing all of us into a new life, inside of "the New Man."

Now our natural habitat is "newness of life."[13] This is the *resurrection-life*, the Life, raised from the dead, of the Son of God, and us in Him. We were "raised with him," in Him.[14] As a spaceship that rises up and leaves the earth, we all ascended inside of The Anointed King when he ascended.

When we speak now, it is from the high position of placement "in Him." So our words carry *weight*, the authority of the Son of God. The Life is already in us. It's new. It's bright—it shines. And that Life is our new Nature.

Our spirit now is alive, dwelling in the light of Life, and it shares the exact nature of God and of The Anointed King. "We are his offspring."[15] Our life is now hidden with The Anointed King in God. We have not yet appeared to the world, though we do manifest for them, from time to time. But our entire internal system is completely different from the old. "All things have become new."

The old creation stumbled badly, and that caused all of the physical world to jolt and crack. But the New Creation has never known such a fall. It didn't fall with Adam. It has never had a split in relationship with God. It lives above, in perfect peace. It breaths out life and glory.

We must give NO SYMPATHY to the dragon. It KNOWS it is outclassed and outmatched compared to us, the risen New Man. It knows.

[Romans 6:9 NASB20] 9 knowing that [The Anointed King],

---

[13] Romans 6:4
[14] Ephesians 2:1-7
[15] Acts 17:28, John 1:12-13, 1John 3:1-2

having been raised from the dead, is never to die again; death no longer is master over Him.

The Anointed King has gone *beyond* death, so that it will never touch Him again. This includes us!

[Romans 6:8 NASB20] 8 Now if we have died with [The Anointed King], we believe that we shall also live with Him,

We share the exact Life with him now, in him. Death can't even find us. We're in a completely different realm. And we are reigning from there, in Life!!! (Ro 5:17).

We're also free from sin, from evil:

[Romans 6:6-7 NASB] 6 knowing this, that our old {Man} was crucified with [Him,] in order that our body of sin might be done away with, so that we would no longer be slaves to sin; 7 for the one who has died is freed [Lit., "made righteous"] from sin.

And we're far above all negative, opposing forces.[16] So the dragon is small to us, as we look from above, through the perspective of the Word, the Truth. He is small, and he is down. Where are we? In newness of Life!!!

[Romans 6:4 NASB20] 4 Therefore we have been buried with Him through [immersion] into death, so that, just as [The Anointed King] was raised from the dead through the glory of the Father, so we too may walk in newness of life.

The newness of life that we walk in, inside of The Anointed King, has no room for the things that tripped up Adam and Eve. We are now of the nature of our Father—God—and ready to walk *exactly* as he does.

The New Creation does not have a sex; it is "neither male nor female":

[Galatians 3:27-28 NASB20, literal] 27 For all of you who were [immersed] into [The Anointed King] have clothed yourselves

---

[16] Eph 1:20-23 & 2:5-6

with [The Anointed King]. 28 There is neither Jew nor Greek, there is neither slave nor free, there is neither male nor female; for you are all one in [The Anointed King] Jesus.

The Anointed King has become your *identity* now.

[Colossians 3:9-11 NASB20] 9 ...you [completely divested yourself of] the old [Man] with its practices, 10 and have put on the new [Man], which is being renewed unto [having] a true knowledge according to the image of the One who created it– 11 in which there is no Greek and Jew, circumcised and uncircumcised, barbarian, Scythian, slave, [or] free, but [The Anointed King] is all, and in all.

So we can identify personally with him. We are his Body. Our fingerprint has his identity. We are One. So what we touch on earth is touched by him. He touches people through us. He does things through *us*.

The New Creation has shed the old one. The Old Man has nothing to do with the New. Its nature and thoughts and ways are different.

So now we must submit our way of thinking, to be cleansed under the constant flow of the Word of God. This allows us to metamorphosize, to rise up and fly. It allows the reality that we are in— the newness—to be seen and felt by the world around us.

We literally transform into all the realities of who we now are, as our mind is renewed by the image of them. This is to be a constant, continual renewing, that enables us to stand strong and call the nations to liberty. New, we are always new.

Chapter 6
The New Creation in Male and Female

[1 Corinthians 6:11 NKJV, emphasis mine] 11 And such were some of you [that is, wayward people, including those who engage in all kinds of sexual perversions]. BUT you were washed, but you were sanctified [Lit., set apart, made distinctive], but you were justified [Lit., made righteous] in the name [or "authority"] of the Lord Jesus and by the Spirit of our God.

Whatever sexual deviation anyone engaged in before entering The Anointed King now no longer exists, except possibly in the memory. We are totally new.

Being born as the new being, totally new, we're similar to Adam just after he was made alive in an earthly body—everything is new for us. We're in the light, with no need to be ashamed, and we don't know anything yet, so we need to learn. The New Creation grows and feeds and learns, as the people who are part of it focus on the image of God that they can see in His Word. We enhance by that; like fire, we grow.

We hear our Father's Word and receive it—choosing to allow it to enter our hearts—and it becomes alive in us, taking shape and form in us as we live it out.[17]

The New Creation does not need law.[18] Its oxygen is grace and truth. By those it can do *anything*. Miracles are the norm for the glorious New Creation, who spans realms. The new, alive spirit *affects* the physical realm, more so than living *in* the physical realm. It leaves its huge footprint in the physical realm.

Actually, trying apply outward, earthly laws is the kryptonite of the New Creation, as that brings an alive person down to the lower, earthly level.[19]

---

[17] 1Thessalonians 2:13
[18] 1Tim 1:9-10
[19] Romans 7, 2Corinthians 3, Colossians 2:20-23

Those in the New Creation are taught to set their focus on Truth, on "things above" (Colossians 3:1-2), of the invisible realm, the "unseen things" (2Corinthians 4:18). In this way, they renew continuously.[20] They're out of the realm of sin already.[21]

By the Word, the New Man knows the context of the temporary period we are in. It learns the end that is coming and why we are here. It discovers that purpose and "suits up" for it. The Old Man has no idea there's an end, or hardly any idea of a beginning. They are just being moved along through history by time, as it passes away.

The earthly "tent" for the New Creation is the bodies of the "saints" (Literally, the "set apart ones"). Those bodies *do have* distinctions such as sex (male or female), ethnicity, etc. Those are low-level distinctions, and temporary, but they are there. So we each have different places or posts to occupy individually, while on earth as foreigners.

Just as the Old Creation must eat—*often*—the New Creation must also. With consumption of the right food we can "grow up in ALL things to him who is the Head," (Eph 4:15) that is, to FULL STATURE. With proper food consumption, we *grow out* of *any* problem, including any addiction or fear, into the glorious stature of the Son of God, while among the world on earth. Earth to us is like a foreign jungle, full of vines and with opposition, but one that we learn to master as we *grow* into *full stature*—*among* the world but *of* our Father.

Tradition says to "try to be good," which is a denial of the Truth that says we are already good. Tradition's way is to hear one or two messages per week and try to do ones best. But the jungle swallows people who try to live like that.

We consume spiritual nourishment by

1) hearing and receiving it,
2) living it,
3) speaking it (privately), and
4) speaking it to others in love—*teaching it*

Every believer needs to engage in all of these because the appetite of your spirit is voracious!

If a lion tries to live like a sitting duck, it will be treated like one.

---

[20] 2Corinthians 3:18
[21] Romans 6:14, 6:2; 1Jon 3:5

24

This has been our way.[22]

Being disconnected from God the Old Man must live by outward laws. Of course, guidelines and established rules (such as traffic laws) are necessary on earth, for order. Common sense and discretion are also necessary. But the Old Man's way—including *all* human religion—is "do this, don't do that" in hopes of being pretty much good.

But that system reveals that, by nature, they are not good. It is a fallen human race, born as slaves to sin.[23] The Law of Moses was given for the purpose of revealing this, that fallen man is utterly desperate, being permanently disfigured internally.[24] No matter how much they try to wiggle free, the more they try, the tighter they feel the bondage that they are in.

The only rescue is God's generous gift of Jesus, his sacrifice and Lordship for people.

The Truth of the Good News ("Gospel") reveals God's generosity in giving Jesus, and what it has done in us: the new nature—a new identity. This is our foundation—we are in The Anointed King. The more we see that Truth about us, the further up and out from the earth we go. We find that we are in the heavenlies, enthroned in The Anointed King. We look down to the earth with eyes of love and extreme power, as the supernatural, New Man.

As our identity becomes clear to us as "the man of steel," we simply walk in it. Do you see how Truth changes our eyes and thinking, so that we live on earth totally differently?

On the foundation of our NEW identity as The Anointed King's dignified Body, we grow by a multitude of Truth the Spirit brings cascading onto us. We receive illumination as the Spirit causes "the eyes of our understanding to be enlightened, so that we may know..." (Ephesians 1:18).

The New Creation shows compassion (that is, "mercy"). It sees through lenses of mercy, through the mercy-glasses of the Good News. This is a great and easy way to view the world—no heaviness, no gravel in our eyes, no lack of hope for people. ☺ Why can we do that? Because we received mercy—that's the only reason we're here, in The Anointed King. It's the only way in.

---

[22] For more Truth and freedom in this area, I recommend to you my book, "Return to Acts Christianity," and my course, "Church in Acts."
[23] Romans 7:14, 3:9
[24] Romans 7:13

[Titus 3:3-5 NKJV] 3 For we ourselves were also once foolish, disobedient, deceived, serving various {strong desires} and pleasures, living in malice and envy, hateful and hating one another. 4 But when the kindness and the love of God our Savior toward man appeared, 5 not by works of righteousness which we have done, but according to His mercy He saved us, through the washing of regeneration and renewing of the Holy Spirit,

[1 Peter 2:9-10 NKJV] 9 But you [are] a chosen generation, a royal priesthood, a holy nation, His own special people, that you may proclaim the praises of Him who called you out of darkness into His marvelous light; 10 who once [were] not a people but [are] now the people of God, who had not obtained mercy but now have obtained mercy.

So having been shown mercy, and staying free from human, religious tradition so that the view of that mercy is not obscured, we *pour out* mercy on everyone around us. This keeps us personally in good shape, not entangled by deceptive, vine-like, jungle-like, predator plants.

For the same reason, the New Creation does not judge fallen humans. We just got out of court, judged completely innocent for free by God's love for us, at Jesus' expense! We can only be happy and thankful. We're joyful in view of this.

The New Creation grows in all things, like God. He's our Dad. These areas of growth affect all of our relationships. We don't look to use people.

So when it comes to male-female interaction, we grow into showing great respect and honor to the opposite sex, giving space and serving one another in selfless love. In the areas in which Adam and Eve failed, we succeed. Our relentless, dogged focus on the image of God in the Truth, frees us from extreme, out-of-whack desires for companionship or beauty.

We have complete access to our Father who is always working. He's working to help us and to save those who haven't heard of Jesus fully. We can interrupt him and he gives us his full attention, and gives us the information we need for whatever area of weakness or vulnerability we may have.

No matter what physical environment you find yourself in on earth, you are first in God. And he is "at work in you" so that you will what he

26

wills.[25] He's working on your inner desires. He is supporting the areas of weakness in our souls, as we rely on him and what the cross of Jesus did for us. After a bit, we find ourselves healed in the area we were weak and break out in full strength, no longer hurt (by addiction or whatever thing it was).

The New Creation thrives on serving. Serving is an expression of love, and its nature is love. What those who came before tried to do by commandment and failed ("Love God and love your neighbor"), the New Creation does from far above, naturally, without thinking. This serving becomes constant in a person's life through "true-knowledge," by the renewing of the mind, so that it is embedded in every aspect of a person's life. All relationships of ours benefit from it.

The New Creation has access to the Wisdom of God, having the Father Himself in them. This wisdom, along with understanding and other benefits from God, helps us conduct ourselves in the world exactly the way our Father would.

---

[25] Philippians 2:13

About the Author

David O'Brien is a joyful husband and a father of two daughters. He serves as regional director in Christ Love Ministries International, alongside his father in faith and mentor, Ap Charles Ndifon. He is also a co-leader for God's People, at the headquarters of Kingdom Embassy Intl. in Rhode Island, USA. He travels both within the United States and abroad to serve.

Also known as The Bondage Breaker, he champions freedom and distinctiveness in the world, through the Living Word of The Anointed King. David has started The Purity Forum and The Purity Alliance, to shine light for today's youth. He also co-founded East West Services, an anti-human trafficking 501c3, whose main effort is the Be The Light Movement for youth: www.BeTheLightMvmt.com.

David is the president of Empower Media Network, "empowering you to empower others" — EmpowerMediaNetwork.com.

David spent years living and serving abroad in Africa and Asia, and he has written several powerful books, including "For Freedom," "In Search of The Bride," "Return to Acts Christianity," "Heal The Sick," and "SHINE - Daughter of God, It Is Your Time."

One of David's favorite accomplishments is this "Supernatural Royalty-Ed" series, which will bring clarity, healing, freedom, joy and beauty for ashes, to so many of God's people.

Life Changing Resources

The Supernatural Purity Ed Series, by David O'Brien

Other Books by David O'Brien
- In Search of the Bride – The King is Looking for The One
- For Freedom – How God Freed You from Slavery
- SHINE – Daughter of God, it is Your Time!
- Heal the Sick – Gospel Healing Training for The New Man
- Return to Acts Christianity
- Jesus The King

Empower Media Network - *EmpowerMediaNetwork.com,* also on YouTube, Facebook, and Instagram
Empowering You to Empower Others!
- Miracle clips, documentaries, and more…!
- The Purity Forum Broadcast, by David O'Brien
- Daily Boost and other programs, by Dr Charles Ndifon
- For Freedom Broadcast, by David O'Brien

Free & Pure to Shine. David's Supernatural Life Coaching:
www.FreeAndPureToShine.com

Other Amazing Resources:
- PSOM.org
- Podcast: Lovely Talk for Lovely Women, by Sonia O'Brien
- Be The Light Podcast, by David O'Brien
- For Freedom Radio, by David O'Brien – ForFreedomRadio.com

TheBondageBreaker.com

BlueDiamondBookhouse.com

29

30

THE PURITY
FORUM

WWW.EMPOWERLIVETV.COM

DAVID O'BRIEN
DAILY - 9:30PM EST
(WED 6:30)

FORFREEDOMRADIO.COM

IT WAS
FOR
FREEDOM...

LIBERATING...

LIFE-GIVING...

DIVINELY
POWERFUL!

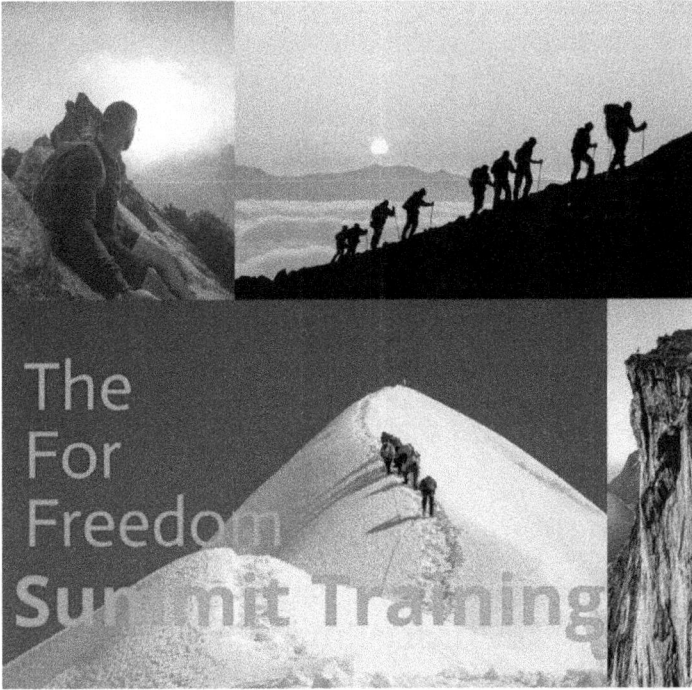

The
For
Freedom
Summit Training

Lovely Talk for Lovely
Women
A Podcast by Sonia O'Brien

On Spotify & Anchor

We welcome your positive feedback!!

If you have been immensely blessed by this work, and if you can, please send your video or written **TESTIMONIAL** to us via

BlueDiamondBookhouse.com
or
info@TheBondageBreaker.com

Thank you!